Help is on the Way

Help is on the Way

A Homeschooler's Guide to Accommodations
for the SAT, ACT, and College

By

Hal & Melanie Young

**Help is on the Way: A Homeschooler's Guide
to Accommodations for the SAT, ACT, and College**

©2018 by Hal & Melanie Young, All Rights Reserved
©2023 by Hal & Melanie Young, Revision and Expansion, All Rights Reserved
Great Waters Press
www.GreatWatersPress.com

If purchased in eBook format, this eBook is not licensed for resale. This license is personal to the original purchaser and may not be sold, loaned, or otherwise transferred to third parties or additional users. Purchaser may make one copy for each member of their immediate household. Additional Licenses should be purchased if you'd like to share this eBook with anyone outside your family. Sample pages may be adapted for your own use, but not resold or posted for download or printed for use by others.

Contact info@greatwaterspress.com for information.

Copying for school or co-op use is strictly prohibited. Each family should purchase their own copy.

No part of this publication may otherwise be published, reproduced, stored in a retrieval system, or transmitted or copied in any form or by any means now known or hereafter developed, whether electronic, mechanical, or otherwise, without prior written permission of the publisher. Illegal use, copying, publication, transfer or distribution is considered copyright infringement according to Sections 107 and 108 and other relevant portions of the United States Copyright Act.

The use of any trademarked names does not imply endorsement or approval by the companies holding those trademarks. This document is intended only to enhance your user experience.

Cover Design by Melanie Young, ©2018.

Contents

A Word	7
A Surprising Place to Be	9
Isn't That Cheating?	11
Diagnosis and Documentation	13
Developing an Educational Plan	15
SAT vs ACT vs CLT	19
Getting Accommodations on the SAT	21
Eligibility	21
Requesting Accommodations	23
What's Next?	25
Getting Accommodations on the ACT	27
Eligibility	27
Requesting Accommodations	27
What's Next?	30
Dealing with Difficult Testing Coordinators	33
What Does Test Day Look Like?	37
Applying to College or University	39
And what about scholarships?	40
The Actual Application Process	40
To reveal or not?	41
Before You Decide	42
Accommodations in College	45
When Things Don't Go Well	46
Better Than You Think	47
Affording All This	49
Expenses for Diagnosis	49

    Expenses for College Admission Exams 49

    College Application Fee Waivers 51

    Financial Aid for College 52

Looking Forward.. 53

Ideal Timeline.. 54

Resources 58

    Resources for SAT, PSAT, PSAT 10, and AP Exams... 58

    Resources for the ACT Exam 59

    Resources for the CLT Exam... 60

    Fee Waiver Resources... 60

    Resources for Educational Plans 61

    Possible Accommodations 61

    Resources for Applying to College 62

    Financial Help with Diagnostic Testing 63

Sample Email to School Board Official.. 64

Sample Simple Educational Plan 66

Sample Detailed Educational Plan (Seldom Necessary) 70

Sample Educational Plan for Medical Accommodations.. 76

Sample Doctor's Letter for Medical Accommodations... 79

Traditionally Organized Transcript 83

Transcript by Subject 85

Other Books by Hal & Melanie Young 86

A Word

Throughout this book, we use the word disability to describe the differences our children have that give them a need for accommodations. We realize many parents aren't comfortable with that word, sometimes we aren't either! God made our children the way that they are and their struggles are as much a part of their stories as their successes. That said, disability is the term you will see again and again as you navigate the process of getting your students the help that they need. In fact, it is the Americans with Disabilities Act that has opened so many doors for our children, requiring all of these organizations to accommodate those differences. Because of that, we hope that you'll overlook it if the word offends you. We mean no harm.

We've navigated these paths ourselves and understand how emotionally loaded all of this can be. We hope that this book will make your task easier and lift some of the burden as you prepare your children to launch into the world. It's been exciting to us to see the Lord's plan for our children take shape and we look forward to hearing of His grace in your lives, as well.

Hal & Melanie

A Surprising Place to Be

Kids surprise you. I remember a day when our most struggling reader was fourteen and I wondered if he'd ever be able to make it in the world. I knew he was bright, but he was still writing like a first grader and his reading was still a little slow to get high school work done. I never dreamed that in five years he'd be at college on a full-ride academic scholarship, elected freshman class president and doing just fine, thank you.

Did all his struggles magically go away? No. He did have a serious academic growth spurt in high school, though. He grew in confidence. His maturity helped him to manage his issues better. Learning got easier.

School was still challenging for him, though, and it was even more challenging to show what he'd learned. He needed help to reach his full potential.

When our children were young, we were strongly encouraged not to allow our children to be "labeled" with any sort of disability. The whole language of "disability" can be unsettling. We were told, too, it would limit them in the future. Coming from an institutional school system, it is understandable why someone might feel that way. On the other hand, the lack of a diagnostic "label" also prevents the child from getting any interventions to compensate for those struggles. And when you homeschool, the social dynamic changes. If you have your child privately tested, no one needs to know but you – until you need someone to know.

One of those times you need someone else to know your child's situation is when your child may be college bound. Frequently by high school, kids with learning challenges are dealing better with their disabilities. Increasing maturity helps them to form work-arounds or to persevere through difficulties. Twice-exceptional kids, those with both a special need and giftedness, may appear able to manage without accommodations and they may even prefer to, but often perform way below their ability level when they do.

That's what happened to one of our children. He managed all right in high school, so we thought he'd probably be okay in college, too. What we didn't realize was how much we were making accommodations for him at home. He was able to get up and move around at will, he could manage his day to keep himself on track, he was able to do all his essays on a computer instead of by hand. When he got to college, he struggled. When we saw his grades and heard his frustrations, we encouraged him to go to the disabilities office at his college and ask to be tested. They diagnosed him with ADHD and offered him some mild accommodations to deal with it.

His other learning disabilities, though, were disregarded because he was able to perform on the tests as well as an average student. "Why complain when you can maintain a solid C average?" they asked. The problem was, and is, that he is not an average student! His intelligence scores showed that his performance should be well above average. He had an "A" intellect held back to "C" performance, like a high-powered sports car driving with the parking brakes set! If we had tested him sooner, before he was able to cope more easily, he would likely have received truly helpful accommodations, as his younger brother did later.

Another child had a medical condition he could easily manage at home, usually without even taking meds. The rigors of college life, though, exacerbated his condition and make coping really difficult. Can you imagine dealing with a migraine while sharing a room with a student who may have friends over or who may be working on some project that requires a lot of light? Pulling together the documentation our son needed led to accommodations that will make college life easier.

Getting accommodations on college admissions tests makes a real difference to kids with learning or medical challenges: It allows them to perform up to their potential and may not only get them into college but may open the door to the scholarships that allow them to afford it. Getting accommodations once they arrive at college can allow them to succeed in a way they might not be able to otherwise. These things make it worthwhile to pursue a diagnosis early and document the accommodations they need to do well in higher education.

Isn't That Cheating?

A lot of us struggle with the whole idea of accommodations. Whenever we speak about the struggles of one of our children, we inevitably have this conversation with someone at the booth afterward:

"I'm just not sure about this accommodations thing. Isn't that cheating?" the concerned mother begins. "Besides, his father doesn't want me to cut him any slack. He says he needs to learn to cope in the real world. And if I did modify his curriculum, how could I still give him credit for the class?"

Look at it this way. If your son lost a leg in an accident, would you consider it cheating for him to use a prosthetic or crutches? Of course not! It's not cheating to help your child overcome a disability which interferes with him doing whatever God has prepared him to do. Your son may have a physical challenge to overcome, or he might have a learning challenge to deal with. Accommodations just level the playing field, so your struggling learner can express the ability you know he has.

I can say that now, but there was a time when it was really hard for me. I remember the day I changed my mind. Our severely dyslexic son had come to me a few months earlier and shared how sad he was that he couldn't compete in our state history museum's essay contests and win money like his brothers. A lightbulb went on in my head and I called the museum outreach director.

"I have a student with a learning disability," I said. "Would it be acceptable for him to dictate his essay?"

She responded that dictating was perfectly all right, so long as the student did his own research and the scribe typed exactly what the student said.

With that guideline, our son composed an essay for the contest...and won first place in our entire state! I will never forget his response. For the first time, he really believed what I'd been telling him – that he was a bright young man who just had a bunch of challenges to deal with. The day he won that award, he grew a determination and confidence that helped him to keep fighting.

Accommodations allow our kids to use the gifts God gave them. My son could never have written that essay by hand. His handwriting was like a first grader's at the time, even though he was in middle school, and writing even a few words was extraordinarily painful. Yet, this wasn't a handwriting exercise. It wasn't a timed test. It was a contest of research and composition, and he composed an essay better than any other student in our state. The accommodation allowed him to demonstrate his ability. That's the kind of difference appropriate accommodations can make.

It's important to ask ourselves, "Why are we teaching our children? What's the point?" Are we going through all this to produce a few boxes of filled-in workbooks and papers full of writing? Or are we homeschooling in order to teach our kids what they need to know before they embark on adult life? If this home education is meant to help them learn what they need, then that's what we need to be focusing on—not whether their worksheets are all completed just like everyone else's.

In the same way, it's important when we evaluate our student's learning that we're evaluating what they've actually learned, not just their test-taking skills. That's why it's not cheating to pursue accommodations on college entrance exams or to use them in their regular learning. It's smart.

Diagnosis and Documentation

Diagnosing and documenting a disability generally requires testing by a professional in the field. Medical issues can be diagnosed by a doctor, but a mere letter is not enough. The report needs to include the results of appropriate tests. Learning, neurological, and psychological disabilities will likely need to be diagnosed by a neurologist or psychologist. This testing can cost anywhere from a few hundred dollars to two or three thousand and will generally take several hours to complete. That can seem intimidating to homeschool families but listen: That testing is important. It's the key that opens the door to accommodations outside your home.

HSLDA is a great resource for finding an evaluator who is friendly to homeschoolers. We strongly recommend HSLDA membership for everyone but *particularly* for families who have children with special needs. We often need to interact with professionals and institutions that may not understand homeschooling or the homeschool law. HSLDA also has a team of Special Needs Coordinators that help members with advice, referrals, and resources. Their department alone is worth the price of membership!

When you arrange testing with the evaluator you choose, make sure that you tell them that you will be applying for SAT or ACT accommodations and you'll need a full report that includes a diagnosis justified by test results, history of the disability, functional limitations, and suggested accommodations.

Testing of any kind can be stressful to a struggling learner. Reassure them that the testing isn't something they have to get a certain grade on or pass. It's more like a doctor checking their height, weight, and blood pressure – it's just a measurement, not a competition. Encourage them that the information you get from the testing may help you understand how to help them succeed more easily.

When you receive the report, check to make sure it includes everything needed and make copies, or better yet, scan it. You'll need copies whenever you apply for accommodations for testing and college.

Many people say not to tell students the results of diagnostic testing. That's up to you, but sometimes results can be an encouragement to them. Too often kids have already diagnosed themselves – as stupid and they think that's why school is so hard. Especially for twice-exceptional kids, who are high intelligence but have learning disabilities, seeing the results may change everything for them. They might understand for the first time that they have what it takes to succeed – they just need to do things differently than other folks and they may need some help along the way.

It's important that we help our kids get comfortable discussing their disability. As our kids approach adulthood, it becomes more important for them to thoroughly understand test results, implications, and accommodations – because when they are out of our homes, they'll have to advocate for themselves!

Developing an Educational Plan

When our children need to interact with the outside educational world, it's intimidating to wade into the battle to get them accommodations. We may be confronted with an entire culture of special needs services and programs with a technical vocabulary of their own. We'll need to learn to sift this education-ese for ourselves.

One common request is for a student's IEP or 504 plan. Unless your student was in an institutional school once, and received accommodations while he was there, he probably won't have one of these plans. What, exactly, are officials asking for?

Testing organizations and colleges will want to know what kind of accommodations a student already receives as a part of their normal school experience. Their assumption is that an accommodation which is needed for normal schoolwork will likely be needed for the test. On the other hand, they assume if a student gets by without an accommodation on an average day, they can probably do without it on test dates.

That logic is debatable for a homeschooler. Our typical day isn't like a typical classroom day. For example, if our kids are free to get up and move around as needed, we don't have to declare formal "extra breaks." In a classroom structure, those breaks may be critically important. So, the question we need to ask is, "What accommodations would my child need in a typical *classroom* situation?" Then we develop an educational plan that outlines those accommodations.

Some organizations you deal with are fine with a letter explaining the kind of accommodations your student receives. That's certainly a lot less stressful than trying to write a formal plan, but having that written plan may open doors with the more skeptical people because it is the kind of document they are accustomed to seeing.

When we first wrote a plan like this, there were few examples online and I wasn't even sure what it should look like. Thankfully, there are now many examples you can look through. We've also included a sample detailed educational plan as well as a simple one in the back of the book, as well. You can learn more about this kind of document under Resources at the end of this book.

Let's talk about each part. You might want to stick a bookmark or finger in the example in the back so you can refer to it as you read through this.

At the top, put your school name and address, like you might for a letterhead.

Then you need identifying information about your child – name, Social Security number, birthdate, grade, school year, which years they needed accommodations (now, remember, that includes things you may not think of as accommodations, such as using a stroller for a preschooler than struggles to walk a long way reading math problems aloud for your late reader), and date of expected graduation.

The next section gives the official diagnosis and information about the tests that support it. You can copy this straight from the report you received from your evaluator. Include the date, evaluator name and credentials, and what specific tests were given. Then list dates on which any previous testing was done.

In the next section, you'll address each of the academic areas in which your student needs accommodation, for example, reading, writing, math, or general schoolwork. In each area, you need to explain their current level of academic achievement, accommodations that may be used, and goals to accomplish over the next year or so.

Although it looks more complicated, it was easiest for me to refer to the testing and the evaluator's words to explain our students' current status. I just transferred test information and quotes from the evaluator onto our plan. You could also use a narrative format and just explain where they are academically.

You will need to establish goals for your student for the next year, outlining the kind of improvements you expect to see.

Finally, you'll want to write out in detail the kind of accommodations your student might need. Be sure to think through what they would need in a normal *classroom* setting as well as what they need at home. If they took a dual enrollment class at the local community college, what kind of accommodations would they need not just to survive, but to do well in that environment?

In the Resources section, there are several links to lists of possible accommodations. I suggest you read through them. You may find accommodations you haven't thought of. Include anything you think might help your child to better succeed because often the accommodations you list in this document will be the ones that are approved for college admission tests and even in the college classroom.

SAT vs ACT vs CLT

The SAT, ACT, and CLT are all college entrance exams that provide a way for college admissions committees to compare students from widely different backgrounds. The exams vary in some significant ways and different students will perform better on one than the other.

The SAT was developed as a college aptitude test. Since the test makers recognized that schools varied in curricula, the goal wasn't to test knowledge, but to test the ability to benefit from a college education. This made the SAT similar in some ways to an IQ test, but more focused on academic ability.

The ACT, on the other hand, was developed as an achievement test for students graduating from high school. It was more focused on showing what the student had learned and how prepared they were for college. Both tests have changed a great deal since then and they are more alike than they used to be, but they still have significant differences.

Originally, colleges on the East Coast and West Coast required the SAT and colleges in the Midwest required the ACT. Later, colleges began accepting either. These days it genuinely doesn't matter which you submit to colleges.

The CLT is a new player. The texts students read and respond to are based on the classic great books instead of the more textbook or research article type of prose found on the SAT and ACT. It is not well-known yet, but it has some advantages. It provides more score detail at the top end of the scale, so a really excellent student may get even better scores on the CLT than they would at on the SAT or ACT. It is likely to allow students to showcase the education they might receive in a school more classically-oriented than most public schools.

There is no downside to taking each of these tests and taking them more than once. Unlike just a few years ago, you can now choose what scores to report to a college even on the SAT. Every college bound student should take the SAT and ACT, preferably twice each and top students should probably also take the CLT if it is convenient.

Practice is very important to score well. Free practice tests are available online (check the Resources section). The best way to practice is to complete a subsection, then read through the answer explanations. It will teach you how the test makers think. One student we know with severe test anxiety did not score highly enough to get into the college she wanted when she first took the SAT. She completed every practice test she could and retook the exam in a couple of months and scored highly enough not just to get in, but to get a scholarship.

Getting Accommodations on the SAT

The College Board is the organization in charge of the SAT, PSAT/NMSQT, PSAT 10, and AP Exams. To get accommodations on any of these tests, you'll need to go through their Services for Students with Disabilities (SSD) department. The good news is that once you are approved for accommodations for one College Board exam, you are approved for all of them except PSAT 8/9 and CLEP exams. For those exams, you'll need to request accommodations from the testing facility directly.

If you go to the College Board site and search on the accommodations process, nearly every page will warn you "Most Students Work with Their Schools." **Those warnings aren't directed at you.** They are trying to cut back on parents doing an end run around their school counselor to receive more accommodations. Homeschool students *must* go directly to the College Board and that's okay – they have a process for us.

Eligibility

The College Board has several requirements in order for a student to be eligible to receive accommodations:

1. A documented disability.
2. The disability would impact taking an exam.
3. A particular accommodation is needed.
4. Accommodations are received on tests at the student's school.

Let's break that down.

The College Board requires that students applying for accommodations have a documented disability such a learning, visual, medical, physical, or motor impairment. That could be anything from ADHD to blindness, diabetes to dyslexia.

You've got to be able to document that disability with a report from a doctor or a psychologist. That report needs to document what testing was done, what the results were, and how that limits the student's activities with regards to schoolwork or testing.

The kind of documentation needed for different disabilities is in the Resources section. Most require a clearly stated diagnosis based on current information (within the past five years, usually) with the student's history of disabilities described. That diagnosis needs to be supported by test results. The student's functional limitations should be included and suggested accommodations should be justified. The evaluator should state their professional credentials.

Now, don't panic when you read all that. When I first read the requirements, I was concerned we'd need to redo all of our son's expensive testing. When I looked back and reread the report we received, though, it included every single thing they requested. These are normal expectations for an educational psychologist!

Now, what do they mean by a disability that would impact taking an exam? A student may have a disability that severely limits life functions but may not impact taking an exam. For example, a student may need help getting to the classroom and to their seat but would not necessarily need accommodations on the exam itself. In order to receive accommodations, the disability has got to impact actually taking the exam. That might include a student with diabetes who needs access to food, testing equipment or medication during test hours or a student with slow processing speed who needs extra time on the test.

There's where the needed accommodations come into play. Documentation will need to show that the student needs accommodations to perform well. Accommodations can be all sorts of different things. Some common ones are extended time, braille or large-print tests, extra breaks, a scribe to record answers, use of a computer, and a reader to read questions. In the Resources section, there is a link to the different accommodations available.

Finally, the College Board requires that the student receive the same kind of accommodations in their own school. This is the one that throws some homeschoolers. The College Board is making the assumption that if the child doesn't need accommodations in their ordinary school setting that they probably don't need them in a college admissions exam either. That's a bit of a leap, perhaps, but it's part of their requirements. They want you to provide some sort of documentation of the accommodations provided in your homeschool.

Don't worry, it's not that hard. If your student were in school, they would have an IEP or 504 plan that would detail how teachers should accommodate the student's disabilities and the school would transmit that information to the College Board. You may not have done that because, well, it seems silly to direct yourself to give accommodations. It's one of those things you need to do, though. You can do the same thing by writing up an educational plan for your child and sending it in. See the section on Educational Plans for help putting this together. Just remember that it's important to include accommodations that you would use if your student were in a classroom environment.

Requesting Accommodations

It can take up to several months to get accommodations approved, so you need to start early. It's good plan to start the process six months or so before the child will take a College Board exam. If you want your child to take the PSAT with accommodations to qualify for National Merit Scholarships, you'll want to start not later than early spring in the sophomore year. If the SAT is the first test you want them to take, you'll need to start in the fall of the junior year.

If this is all new to you and your child needs to take an exam as quickly as possible, don't give up. Just check the deadlines for accommodations applications for each test date (link in the Resources section) and get the documentation in as quickly as possible.

An application for accommodations contains these parts:

- The Student Eligibility Form – link in the Resources section
- Documentation of Disability
- Student's Educational Plan
- Other Information

Download and print out the Student Eligibility Form at the link. Choose "actual size" when printing. Enter the student's information in sections 1-6. In section 7, list your homeschool name and address, not the school where they'll take the exam. In section 8, you'll put the CEEB code for homeschooling, 970000. Enter sections 9-11.

Section 12 of the form is the place to actually request accommodations. Choose what your student would need to truly excel, not just the bare minimum they would have to have. These tests can open a lot of doors for your child. Do your best to make sure they have what they need to show what they are capable of. If there are several different options that address the same need, choose the one you believe would work best or is closest to what you do at home. For example, for a child with dysgraphia who normally uses a computer for essays at home, you might request a computer, but for a child who doesn't type yet or who is accustomed to dictating essays, you might do better to request a scribe. If you have a child that has written reversals that may cause them to bubble in the wrong place, you may want to request a large answer sheet or a scribe, as well. A student whose medical disability makes it difficult to write should ask for a scribe so they can concentrate on the work, not the pain.

Do keep in mind that they are not allowed to move on to the next text or leave the room until all the given time has expired. Requesting 100% more time can make for a very long day and very long test sessions.

Section 13 is where you'll verify that these are the kind of accommodations you've been using in their regular schooling. Of course, that's the norm, to give a student the help he needs to succeed every day, even if it is less formal at home than it would be in a national exam.

In section 14, you'll mark the disability that is impacting their performance on the exam.

Section 15 is where you tell them what kind of documentation and educational plan you are sending in. I would highly recommend that you create a formal plan right now, before even you start this process, and bubble in the sections for "Current Formal Written Plan/Program" and "Student is Homeschooled." Then enter the date the first plan was approved. If you have noted in your lesson plans accommodations provided since they were 3rd grade, for example, then put that date.

Finally, enter the name and credentials of the evaluator or doctor who wrote the report you will send in, diagnosing the disability for which you are claiming accommodations, and then the specific tests used.

Leave section 16 blank.

For guidance on the documentation needed and the student's educational plan, see the parts of this book dedicated to those.

Assemble a packet (a large manila envelope works well) with the Student Eligibility Form, a copy of your latest disabilities evaluation, a copy of the Student Educational Plan, and a letter sharing any other pertinent information. Make copies of everything you send in and keep them on file. Mail it Priority Mail or Return Receipt Requested so that you can make sure it was received. The current address is found in the Resources section.

What's Next?
Within a couple of months, you should receive a letter that details exactly what accommodations are allowed for each test and includes an SSD number. When the student registers for the SAT, he'll answer yes to the question about accommodations and enter this number when prompted. The form may only allow seven digits, which is what remains when the leading zeros are deleted from the SSD number.

The admission ticket generated at the end of registration should state that accommodations will be offered. If not, contact the Services for Students with Disabilities office immediately.

If you are registering before accommodations have been approved, perhaps to avoid paying a late fee, check the admission ticket as the day approaches to make sure that accommodations are added to the ticket.

Be sure to contact the guidance counselor at the test center where the student will be testing to see if they have received notice of the accommodations and if your student will be testing on the normal test day or not. Some accommodations will require that a student be tested separately or on two days. Those accommodations usually mean testing will happen apart from the usual test administration, but not always. Communication is critical.

If your child will be taking the PSAT or AP exams, you will need to register them with a local high school that administers those tests. Make a copy of the accommodations letter you receive and give it to them when you register. Again, stay in close contact with the testing coordinator at the school and ensure that they are prepared to give your student the accommodations needed. Sometimes that will mean that they test on a different day than other students, often alone with a teacher or in a small group.

Finally, test scores will NOT reflect the use of accommodations, so you are free to disclose the disability, or not, on college applications.

Getting Accommodations on the ACT

The ACT organization administers the ACT college admissions test, as well as a few lesser known tests. ACT's information on accommodations can be easily found with an online search, but the level of information seems to vary between large-print infographics with little information and abstruse documents full of education-ese. This summary should help.

Eligibility

Like the College Board, ACT requires that students requesting accommodations:

1. Have a diagnosed disability that substantially impacts life activities.
2. Request accommodations that are reasonable and appropriate.

Disabilities which may receive accommodations include learning disabilities, ADHD and related disorders, psychiatric disorders, visual or hearing impairment, autism spectrum disorders, speech and language disorders, medical conditions, and traumatic brain injuries.

Accommodations offered are similar to those offered for the SAT but we have found that accommodations for learning disabilities are a bit harder to qualify for and accommodations for medical disabilities a bit easier. Accommodations like extended time, extra breaks, computer or scribe, and large print booklets are available.

Requesting Accommodations

Unlike the SAT, the first thing you will do to prepare to take the ACT exam with accommodations is to register for the test. The ACT *will not* accept an accommodations request unless the student is registered for a test. Indicate the need for accommodations when asked and select the type of accommodations needed. There is a link to an infographic in the Resources section to help you know what kind of accommodations to request.

You'll receive an email with instructions to contact your school guidance counselor to complete the request. That does not apply to most homeschoolers since we do not have disability documentation on file at a school.

Instead, like the College Board, you'll need their form and documentation:

- Request for ACT-Approved Accommodations – link in the Resources section
- Documentation of Disability
- Student's Educational Plan or an Exceptions Statement – link in the Resources section
- A copy of your Admission Ticket or confirmation email that the student has registered for the ACT
- Other Information

Start on this early. Although the deadline for submitting documentation is the late registration deadline for the registered test date, it is unwise to leave it that late if you can help it.

Download and print the Request form linked in the Resources section. Enter student information and the testing date the student is registered for. If not registered, stop and do that, then come back to the form. Yes, this is frustrating, since you might decide not to use this test if the student doesn't get adequate accommodations, but that's the way it works with the ACT.

Enter the type of accommodations needed and if English support is not needed, skip to section G. Enter the *specific diagnosis* found on the disability evaluation you received when your child was tested.

In section H, select either "Official Accommodations Plan" or "Exceptions Statement" depending on whether you want to present an educational plan, as outlined in a different part of this book, or fill out their form explaining the accommodations you give your student in your homeschool. You will likely not receive any accommodations that the student does not already receive at home, so go into detail.

If you've been offering accommodations throughout high school and before, as I hope you have, select the appropriate answers.

Section I is where you will select the accommodations needed. The accommodations in the first portion are typically offered on a normal test day when everyone else is tested. The second group of accommodations are usually offered in a student's school, so you will need to work with the local school that administers the ACT for your child to be tested separately.

If you request any of those Special Testing accommodations in the second group, you will need to take the form to the high school hosting the ACT for which the student is registered and ask their Testing Coordinator to fill out sections J and K sign the form.

You, the homeschool parent, will sign under L, even though it says Test Coordinator, but you will need to include a letter stating that you are a homeschool teacher and are the proper person to sign the form.

The Exception Form gives you space to detail the accommodations your student receives

Another possible inclusion in the application is the Teacher Survey Form (link in the Resources section), which you can fill out as the homeschool teacher. You can also ask other teachers in your child's life, such as music or co-op teachers, to fill it out.

Make a copy of the documentation you have of your student's disability and of your student's educational plan. You can find the ACT's requirements for that documentation in the Resources section.

You will need to bundle the form, the documentation of disability (usually a testing report by an educational psychologist or a detailed letter from a doctor, see the example at the end), either the student's Educational Plan or the Exceptions Statement, the Teacher Survey Form, if used, and a letter stating that you are signing as a homeschool teacher and sharing any additional material you believe is important. You can either email the bundle or mail it in to the address found in the Resources section.

If you mail the information in, send it in a large envelope by Priority Mail or Return Receipt Requested so you can be sure they received it.

What's Next?

That's one of the problems with ACT Accommodations. Sadly, notification of accommodations letters are *not* sent to students or homeschool parents, but only to the school where the student will be testing. That means it is vital that you stay in contact with them and request that they give you a copy of the Decision Notification, which they can access through the Test Accessibility and Accommodations System. Until you have seen that, you won't know whether the student will be testing on the normal test day or separately at the school on a different day. Checking in on this can be annoying to school test coordinators, but it's vital. Be polite but be persistent.

There is a document with preparation directions for students who will be testing with Special Testing accommodations linked in the Resources section. If you are requesting exam materials in a different format, such as braille or large print, you can order practice materials in the same format (link in the Resources section).

Test scores do not record the use of accommodations, so you may disclose the disability, or not, as you wish, on college applications.

Getting Accommodations on the CLT

The CLT is a new college admissions exam, so their procedures are not as detailed as those of the College Board and ACT. They have issued some guidance, though.

The CLT requests that you submit a request for accommodations at least eight weeks in advance. They require that disabilities cause functional limitations in high school education. Some of the disabilities for which they allow accommodations are ADHD, learning disorders, visual impairment and blindness, hearing impairment and deafness, physical disorders, head injuries, psychiatric disorders, autism spectrum disorders, communication disorders, and tic disorders.

They ask that you submit a letter detailing exactly which accommodations you are requesting and either a current IEP or 504 Plan or a diagnostic testing report. I am assuming they would accept an educational plan, as well, but they don't say so.

The accommodations available on the CLT include mp3 test format, visual magnification (enabled by increasing the size of the font on screen), braille exam (includes all graphs and figures), signed exam, reader, written instructions, signed instructions, additional time, and appropriate seating. Please note that the CLT is administered on a computer, so some accommodations will be different.

Dealing with Difficult Testing Coordinators

Many times, perhaps most of the time, you'll find that school guidance counselors chose that career because they wanted to help students and they are glad to help yours, too. It helps if you are always polite and gracious, recognizing that they have a full workload and that working with homeschool students may seem like an imposition to them. Our experiences have been largely positive.

Every once in a while, though, you hit a brick wall. It's happened to us a couple of times. Once a test coordinator told us that homeschool students were not allowed to take the PSAT at their school at all, since the test day was a regular school day. Another time, a test coordinator told me that she was sorry, but they would not be able to provide the requested accommodations for an AP Exam because they'd have to hire someone to come in and do it and they couldn't do that. Both were wrong, but what do you do?

First, try to work with the coordinator. Ask if there is anything you can do to help? If an additional proctor is needed, would it help if you provided one? That solved the problem for us several times. I asked a friend if she'd be willing to proctor in return for a favor I could do for her. Another time, I hired a college student of our acquaintance to serve as a proctor. It's not ideal to have to go to that expense, but it was important enough to us that he be able to take the test to go the extra mile.

If school officials are not helpful, sometimes private school officials will work with you. It's especially important in the case of private schools to offer to help as much as you are able. Many private schools genuinely do not have extra resources, so providing a proctor may enable them to provide the testing you need. Some may ask for an extra fee. They are not really supposed to do that, but it may be worth it to you to just pay it.

If that doesn't work or if there is no private school available, call the Services for Students with Disabilities office at the College Board or the ACT office that handles disabilities. The phone numbers are listed in the Resources section of this book. They have a lot more sway over school testing coordinators than you do, since they can prevent schools from acting as testing centers. They are also able to explain the law to the testing coordinator. Again, be polite. They will be more likely to go to bat for you if you are easy to work with.

If school officials are still not cooperating, or if it is an issue that the testing authorities can't help you with, go directly to the elected school officials in your district. In our area, the Board of Education is elected to oversee the schools and their budget. In your area, it might be the School Board, the Superintendent of Schools, or something else entirely, but in most areas, there is someone who actually answers to the voters. That is the person you want to talk to.

In the case where I was told homeschoolers could not take the PSAT at our local school, I contacted the school board member of my own political party. I reminded her that we paid property taxes to support the school system even though we educated our children at our own expense. I explained that homeschoolers have no alternative but to go through the school system for these tests and I asked for her help. At the end of this book is a sample email to give you an idea of what to say.

I received an email from the School Board member the next day saying she would check into it and one a few days later telling me to expect to hear from the district testing coordinator that afternoon and to let her know if I didn't or if the problem was not resolved to my satisfaction.

It was amazing how quickly things changed after that! The district and school testing coordinator contacted me immediately and not only allowed our son to test but changed the policy for the entire school district for all homeschoolers. When nothing else will help, the key is to deal with elected officials. They are concerned about losing votes and bad publicity and most know that homeschoolers tend to be an electorate you don't want to upset.

It's best to try to maintain a good relationship from the beginning. If we are unfailingly pleasant and easy to work with, most school officials will be glad to help us. If they aren't, though, don't give up. It's worth the effort to fight for your child's rights.

What Does Test Day Look Like?

Each of our kids has been nervous about what test day would look like with accommodations. No teenager wants to be called out and have people think they are weird. Every time, test day has been a pleasant surprise!

On the day of the test, which may or may not be the same one everyone else tests on, your student will show up at the local high school and go directly to the school office, telling them, "I am supposed to meet Ms. Blank for testing." They will call the test administrator to the office and they'll direct your child to the testing room.

They will typically need sharp #2 pencils, an approved calculator (be sure to get one that is on the approved list on the test company's website), water or a drink, a snack, and meds or other needed equipment. They can NOT use their phone during the test at all, not even as a calculator. In fact, their phone should either be left in the car or turned off entirely and put in the bottom of their bag.

Most of the time, our kids who needed accommodations have tested one-on-one with a teacher, even if testing on a national test day when other students are testing. Every time, the person assigned to test our kids have been wonderful! I think they must ask for volunteers, "Anybody want to test a homeschool student who needs accommodations?" because the test administrators have usually even been positive toward homeschooling! Each teacher we've had has been kind, understanding, and respectful of our child's needs. This is not something you need to stress about! In fact, one of our daughters was so grateful for their kindness that she took them flowers on the last day.

Remind them that there will be problems they can't do and problems that almost no one can do because that's the only way to get a full range of scores and that it's okay, they just need to try every problem that they can.

Encourage your kids to take the breaks they are offered and to use the approved accommodations so that they can truly show what they're capable of.

If your student is receiving extended time, it's either going to be a long day or take more than one day. Be sure you allow for that – with extra snacks and planning. Our kids were totally wiped out after testing, too, so don't plan a busy afternoon or evening afterward.

Our kids were so worried about what it would be like testing with teachers they'd never met, but it was always much better than they feared. Don't worry!

Applying to College or University

Every time one of our children is a senior in high school and we start doing college applications, I am stunned at how much time it takes. It's like a part time job for both of us! When you have a child with special circumstances, you'll need to start even earlier and allow a lot of time.

The first step is research. When we applied to college, back when dinosaurs walked the earth, most kids applied to one college or at most, two or three. These days, though, more students are going to college and it's a lot more competitive and less predictable. Most counselors recommend students apply to six to eight colleges. If your student will need financial aid to manage college, he may need to apply to even more.

A student's list of possible colleges needs a balance of safeties, matches, and reaches. A safety school is one where he's sure to be accepted (an academic safety) and/or he's sure to be able to afford (a financial safety). The best safeties are both. Every student needs to apply to one or two safeties that they'd be happy to attend. How do you know if it's an academic safety? You can look up a college on the College Board site (see the Resources list) and see the percentage of students they admit and their range of average SAT scores. If they either admit the vast majority of students who apply, or your student's SAT score is in the upper range of their SAT scores, that is an academic safety. Any college that admits less than 20% or so of applicants is a reach for everyone, though.

A match school is a college where your student's credentials look like those of other admitted applicants. If they're in that mid-range of college admissions test scores, the school may be a match for them.

A reach school is one where the student falls at or below the bottom of the mid-range of scores, or else the school is so selective that it's a reach for everyone – think Ivy League and top 20 schools.

Your student needs one or two dream schools (the reaches), one or two safeties, and a lot of matches.

And what about scholarships?

It's helpful to remember that scholarships are a recruitment tool – not a prize for the highest score. Colleges use these awards to lure the students they want to add to their incoming class, just a like a football coach recruiting for his team. The problem is, you don't know what the academic "team" is trying to build!

One of our sons received a better scholarship from an elite, top-15 private college, than he did from our local state university. It was cheaper for him to attend the prestigious liberal arts college than to live at home and commute to the big public campus nearby!

Why was that? Well, he wanted to major in politics and economics, and both departments were overcrowded at our state university. Their academic "team" didn't need more economics students! Maybe they needed more agriculture majors or someone in music education or an aspiring physicist. It didn't reflect on the strength of our son's application, but on the needs of the college.

Since you don't know what's going on behind the recruiting decisions, you'll need to apply to a range of colleges for the best chance of scholarships. Be aware that scholarship deadlines are early – as early as the first of October in some places – so start your research in the summer before their senior year *at the latest*.

The Actual Application Process

Many colleges participate in either the Common App or Coalition App, organizations that allow you to enter the information common to all applications just once and then customize each application to the school. We highly recommend you use these if available. Some schools will require that you use their own application, though. Regardless, if your child needs accommodations for tests and schoolwork, you should give them accommodations for applications as well, typing for them, helping them with spelling, etc. A lot of college applications are complicated and even a neuro-typical student usually needs help to get them done.

The essential parts of a college application are the application itself, the essay, the transcript, and at least two recommendation letters (this may vary by college). A parent-produced transcript is completely acceptable, but you need to follow standard conventions. A transcript should be one side of one sheet only, should include the name of the school, identifying information for the student, short course titles and grades, the GPA, or grade point average, and a self-certifying statement and signature of the school administrator. The GPA may be unweighted or you may include both an unweighted GPA and weighted one, giving extra point values for honors and AP classes. For further information on how to do a transcript, see the Resources section. Two sample transcripts have been included, one in traditional format and one organized by subjects, which may be helpful to minimize an unusual high school path. We used that format for one of our students who became gravely ill in high school and had to do one year's work over two years' time and graduate late.

Recommendation letters need to be written by at least one person who can speak to the student's academic ability and at least one who can speak to their character. Those might be co-op teachers, online teachers, coaches, or club advisors.

To reveal or not?

It's really up to the student whether or not to reveal the disability in the application process. One of our sons felt like his learning challenge was so integral a part of who he was, it needed to be a part of his application essay to be authentic. He wanted to show how his disability had inspired him to work harder and to push through to succeed academically. Another student might not want it to be discussed or to enter into the college's decision. It really doesn't matter either way as long as it's not referenced as an excuse, but an explanation.

One of our students was told by an admissions officer, "My desk is covered up with high test scores. I want to know what makes you *different*." That's why the essay may be the most important part of the application. It's your introduction to the admissions committee, the only part of the application that really lets them get to know you as a person. Take some time and brainstorm what it is you want them to know about you. Tell them a story from your life that illustrates those things. It is perfectly acceptable for parents, teachers, or mentors to read the essay, make suggestions, and point out errors that need to be corrected. This is an important piece of writing—take it seriously.

All contact with the college before the admissions decision should be made by the student. Colleges are experiencing an epidemic of helicopter parents and they imagine that homeschool parents will be even worse. That means you can't be. You have to step back and let the student do it. That's especially hard with our special needs kids. We've protected them for a long time and it's hard to let them step up and be adults, but now's the time. They have to be able to do it to survive at college. That means if you visit a college, the student enters first, introduces himself, then introduces you. If you need information from a college, the student should make the call. You can help them to get ready by talking through these situations in advance and role-playing different possibilities.

Before You Decide

If you started early, your student may have a handful of acceptance letters before Thanksgiving. Rejoice, but remember you need more information before you make your final decision—and come what may, that decision needs to be formalized with the college by "National Decision Day," May 1st.

This is more complicated when challenges come into play and there's a need for accommodations. The Americans with Disabilities Act (ADA) and Section 504 of the Rehabilitation Act of 1973 require colleges to provide accommodations, but honestly, some of them are much better at it than others. It's important to consider that when you're deciding where to go.

The first thing to do is contact the college's office of Disability Support Services and let them know that you've been admitted, you have a diagnosed disability, and you'd like to talk to them. You can make an appointment to talk over the phone if visiting is too expensive, but if at all possible, we'd recommend you both visit the college before a final decision. Do your best to know for sure where they ought to go.

When you meet with Disability Support Services or before you talk with them on the phone, they'll need a copy of the same disability documentation that you used to get accommodations on college admissions test – your evaluator's report and your educational plan. In all meetings at the college, it's fine for parents to be present, but they need to take a back seat and let the student lead the way. Don't be antagonistic or demanding going in; you need to build healthy relationships because your child will have to work closely with these folks for four years. Instead, ask questions: How can you help me succeed? I'm concerned about taking notes, is there help for that? Listen carefully to both what they offer and their attitude toward helping. Here are some of the accommodations they might offer:

- Private or small group testing
- Extended time on assignments and testing
- Scribe (limited) or computer-use instead of handwriting
- In-class assignments may be done out of class
- Audiobook textbooks or a text reader and text files for textbooks
- Tutors
- Spelling aids
- Ungraded grammar and spelling
- Another student to take notes for you (and they can do it so that the student doesn't know who they are taking notes for).
- Voice recorder for recording lectures
- Accessible room
- Special meals or access to a kitchen
- Single room
- Assistant for needed tasks
- Class substitutions
- Priority registration so classes can be grouped geographically or by time
- Parking exemptions to park closer or have a car on campus at all
- Permission to have food, drink, or meds in class
- Excused absences above the normal limit
- Accommodating your service dog in class and the dorm

Use the information they share to figure out whether that college will be able to meet your needs or not. Some colleges are known for being great at this, others seem to do only the bare minimum. You need to know that before you decide.

Accommodations in College

This chapter is written to the student, since this is their show!

One of the most critical things you can do to be successful academically is to develop relationships with the people who will come alongside you day by day – your professors and the people in disability services.

Before you register for classes, ask your disability coordinator which of the professor choices for each class are best at working with students with disabilities. Once you register for the course, your disability coordinator should email your needed accommodations to each professor.

This is really important: Before the drop/add period (when you can freely change classes) is over, you need to visit each professor during their office hours. I know this sounds incredibly awkward, but it's not. Instead, it will make a great impression on your professor that will help you in the future.

During the office visit, first express your excitement over studying the material and doing as well as possible. Only after you've introduced yourself and done that, share that you have a disability and that they should have received an accommodations letter from the disability office. Tell them that you just wanted to find out how all that would work in their class. Assure them that you just want to be able to do your very best.

This meeting with your professor will usually let you know if they are willing to work with you or not. If they are resistant or hostile, **drop the class** and look for a better choice for this semester. Especially in the first year or two, you will have enough to do to get your feet under you academically without having to deal with a professor who doesn't want to give you the accommodations you need to be successful.

Sometimes problems don't show up until you've been in class for a while. If that happens, drop in to see your disability support coordinator. This person is your go-to when it comes to problems your disability may cause you. Their job is to be your advocate and to help you succeed. Be extra nice to them, they have a lot of power in your life.

Most professors are glad to help in any way that they can, especially if you prove yourself to be a faithful student, coming to class on time every day, doing the assigned work, paying attention, and learning the material. They love to help students like that—frankly, they're rare, and if you develop that sort of work ethic, your professor will be your biggest ally. If you goof around and don't do what you are supposed to do, though, you will find them unwilling to go out of their way to help you. Remember – your disability is an explanation, but not an excuse.

One of our sons remembers a professor who was a real hardnose. He locked the door at class time so students couldn't enter late. He would not read emails from students and accepted no excuses. Then our son was bit by a poisonous spider and spent the night in the emergency room. He had no alternative, so emailed the professor in the hopes he'd read it. He not only read it, but excused him from class with no penalty. Why did he disregard his own rules? As the professor told our son, he'd been faithful to attend class prepared to discuss the readings time after time. That teacher was willing to go the extra mile because he had proven himself to be a good student.

When Things Don't Go Well

Sometimes, even when you're doing your job, a class just isn't a good fit for you. Some professors just do not want to give students accommodations. One of our sons had a professor who told him outright, "I don't believe that anyone as bright and well-spoken as you are has a learning disability. I refuse not to grade your spelling." Ouch. This son is severely dyslexic and dysgraphic and yes, twice-exceptional. He's very intellectually gifted, but he does need help to succeed in a college environment. His accommodations letter states that he should not be graded on spelling. This professor, though, was elderly, near retirement, and tenured. She simply didn't care what she was supposed to do and there really wasn't much anyone could do about it.

What do you do in a situation like that?

Drop the class. If it's still within the drop/add period, drop the class and go with a different professor or a different course entirely. You can usually take a class another semester with someone else. This is really the best option, and that's why it is so vitally important to meet with the professor before drop/add is over.

Ask your disability support person to intervene. Sometimes the disability office can help a professor to understand the importance of accommodations for your success.

If the drop/add date has passed, ask the registrar to let you drop the course anyway. Sometimes the disability support people can help you to get an exception and do this. You may be able to add another course in its place, but that is rare – and it's hard, since you'll be starting so much later than everyone else.

Appeal to the Faculty Curriculum Committee to substitute another course in the place of this one. This is what our son ended up doing since the professor who refused to help was the only one teaching the second-year course that he needed. His first-year professor had worked with him and he'd done fine with the subject; this professor clearly would not. The faculty committee gave him a list of courses to chose from to substitute for the required course.

Tough it out. Sometimes you'll have no choice but to tough it out. Our sons have done that, too. If you have to do this, take advantage of everything you can that might help. Ask your disability coordinator for all the accommodations that aren't dependent on the professor, such as a student to take notes for you, a voice recorder for class, assigned tutors, and taking exams in the disability office. Also take advantage of the help available to all students: the professor's office hours (to ask questions), supplementary instruction meetings (SI, often hosted by grad students), campus tutoring center, campus writing center, and extra credit assignments. Go to the professor and ask for extra assignments, too.

Sometimes you'll work and work and work and *still* get a B- when you could have gotten an A with the proper accommodations. If so, you just have to trust the Lord through it and keep going. They won't all be like that. And even if they were, people with a B- average get the same degree the A students do.

Better Than You Think

The likelihood is, though, that things are actually going to be better than you think. Our son that struggled the most in our homeschool received his college's top academic scholarship. There was a time he thought he would never even be able to go to college! Once he was there, he found out that professors love students that love to learn. He had a few professors that were a problem, like the one in the last section, but most were glad to work with him. He worked hard, a lot of times longer and harder than his friends, and earned good grades. He made the Dean's List and the President's List. He was elected president of his class. He was able to get a grant to start a business through his college's venture lab. It was more than he ever dreamed possible.

You've got to take the first step, though. You've got to put yourself out there and do what it takes to get admitted to college in the first place. That means you've got to work hard in high school, so your parents can produce a good transcript for you. That means you are going to have to do what it takes to get accommodations on the SAT and ACT – mostly that means your parents have got a lot of paperwork (and possibly expensive testing) to take care of. You've got to practice for the college admissions exams so that you do as well as possible. You've got to apply, which means a lot of complicated applications and essays. The reward, though? You can use the gifts God gave you to do whatever He calls you to do. We know adults who were struggling learners who are now pastors, professors, engineers, doctors, artists, entrepreneurs...all kinds of things. You can do whatever the Lord has gifted you to do. You just have to get started and do the work to get ready.

Affording All This

Most homeschool families are not wealthy, and it can seem impossible to afford the expensive testing, admissions test fees, score report charges, and application fees. Honestly, it is pretty expensive. The good news is that the rewards can be huge – scholarships, a better career path, and more. Plus, there is help available for many of us.

Expenses for Diagnosis

If the disability diagnostic testing you need is not possible for you to afford, contact HSLDA Compassion, formerly known as the Homeschool Foundation. They give grants to homeschool families in need – they helped us. You'll need to show that you've been homeschooling at least a semester, you have a homeschooled child between 6 and 19, you have legal custody of that child, and you have significant financial need. Be sure to follow up and send them the receipts afterward. We had a big health crisis shortly after we received a grant and totally forgot to do that, which caused some confusion.

Expenses for College Admission Exams

When it gets to be time to register for college entrance exams, like the SAT and ACT, if you meet certain requirements, you can apply for a fee waiver. Don't be afraid to do this because a fee waiver can save you a fortune in several different areas. Let's take a look at how to apply and the benefits you receive.

In order to qualify for fee waivers, both the College Board and the ACT require that your family would be eligible for free or reduced price meals if you were a public school family. That does *not* mean that you need to apply for any programs with the government whatsoever! You just have to be within those income guidelines and they are fairly generous if you have a lot of children. You can check your eligibility at the link in the Resources page under Fee Waiver Resources.

If your income falls within those guidelines, print out a copy of that page of the guidelines, and make a copy of the first page of your tax return. Feel free to mark out social security numbers, we do. Also print out a copy of the

Explanation of Fee Waivers from College Board in case your guidance counselor is not sure whether homeschoolers may receive fee waivers. They can!

Call over to your local high school and ask to speak to the Guidance Counselor department. Tell the receptionist that you are a homeschool parent who needs to talk to the guidance counselor in charge of SAT and ACT fee waivers. Ask when would be a good time to come in.

When you go into the school, report directly to the main office first and tell them you are a homeschool parent who needs to talk to a guidance counselor. They may require you to show them your driver's license or to be issued a pass. Then go to the Guidance department.

Explain to the guidance counselor that you are a homeschool parent who needs to get both an SAT and ACT fee waiver and that the guidelines said that you were supposed to get the fee waivers from them. Show them your tax return, the guidelines, and the SAT and ACT explanations. Once or twice, they've asked to keep the documents, but they usually do not. Explain that you'll add the homeschool CEEB code (970000) yourself to the form, so they don't need to add their school code. You may receive up to two fee waiver forms for each of the ACT, SAT, and SAT subject tests. If you student is a junior, you should take only one ACT form since they do expire unless you are registering for the fall test before school is back in session. Do be sure you get the guidance counselor's name and contact info because you may need it in registration.

Once you are home, you can register online with the code on the fee waiver. There is no need to send anything in. Using a fee waiver to register for the ACT or SAT opens up some great benefits that will save you a lot of money.

For the ACT, it will save you registration fees, which can be $50 or more, for the exam or for the exam with writing. You will qualify for up to six free score reports to colleges when you register, plus 20 more later, saving $13 each. Registering with a fee waiver also allows you to add Kaplan Online Prep Live to your order at no charge; this is a pricey practice program you can use to prepare for the ACT. You can also receive fee waivers for up to four college applications.

For the SAT, registering with a fee waiver will save you registration fees for the exam or for the exam with writing, saving $47 or more, plus unlimited free score reports to colleges, worth $12 each, and no late registration fee. You get the Question and Answer Service or Student Answer Service free, which helps you know how to improve your score. You can also take two SAT subject tests free. The fee waiver provides you with a fee waiver for the PROFILE, a financial report required by some colleges before granting financial aid as well as four college application fee waivers. The great thing about the SAT fee waiver is that once you register once with a fee waiver, it automatically adds all the benefits to your account so you don't have to go back to the guidance counselor.

I was unable to find any reference to fee waivers for the CLT exam.

Get all the fee waivers and benefits you qualify for. It can save you hundreds of dollars.

College Application Fee Waivers

College application fees can vary from free to more than a hundred dollars each. If your child is applying to 8 or more colleges, that can really add up. The good news is that when you register with a fee waiver for the SAT or ACT, you also qualify for college application fee waivers.

If you apply to college through the Coalition App or Common App (see the Resources section), you can usually just state that you qualify for an SAT or ACT fee waiver and your college application fees will be automatically waived for most colleges.

For colleges that want a physical application fee waiver, you may print out four of them from your College Board account. If you need more physical fee waivers, which is unlikely, you can print our four ACT application fee waivers and four guidance counselor association fee waivers (see the Resources section) and take them (with your tax return again!) to the local high school for the guidance counselor to sign. The counselor is going to be a lot more patient with you if you fill out all you can on the forms before you bring them in.

Financial Aid for College

In fall of the senior year, as you are getting all the college application forms done, you also need to go ahead and apply for financial aid. If you have much older children, you might be surprised to learn that you can now complete the FAFSA in the fall using financial data from the previous tax year. You'll need to complete the FAFSA for nearly all colleges to receive any financial aid at all, including scholarships.

One question which causes a lot of concern for many homeschool families is the one where it asks for the value of any businesses you own. Please note that does not include family owned businesses with less than 100 employees. I've linked to the explanation of that in the Resources section under Resources for Applying to College.

The FAFSA allows you send results to ten colleges at one time. If you need to send to more than ten, include ten, and submit the form, then do a correction of the form with additional colleges added instead of the original ten, and submit again.

Some colleges, particularly the Ivy League schools and other elite colleges, require you to also fill out the PROFILE, a financial aid application by the College Board. The FAFSA is free, but the PROFILE charges a fee, so you don't need to do it unless one of your colleges requires it. If you have an SAT fee waiver, you may also complete the PROFILE free.

Most importantly, tell your child not to fall in love with a college until they've seen the financial aid package!

Looking Forward

Most of our friends talk about how sad they are when their children leave home for college and I get that. It can be scary, particularly when it's the child that you've worried about and protected for so long. In the end, though, it's an incredibly happy thing – a time you've been working toward all their lives. There truly is no greater joy than to see your children walk in the truth, especially when you can't make them anymore.

We've loved our relationship with our adult kids. It's been interesting to see our relationships transform from strictly parent-boss and child-follower into a more even brother and sister in Christ relationship. It's been one of the great joys of our lives.

Now, expect to get a lot of calls for advice and help as they first move away. You may still need to walk through completing some assignments with your struggling learner at college. They might need help proofreading papers or brainstorming for projects. Encourage them to use a calendar app to keep track of all their assignments. Struggling learners can't afford to wait until the last minute to get assignments done.

Those calls for help tend to grow less and less as each of our children has made the way through college, but we still talk often, as we do with all our adult kids. I hope that never stops.

Don't dread your child stepping up and taking his place in the world. This is what you've prepared them for. It's not the end, it's a beginning. Your relationship will change, but there's a lot of happiness yet to come!

Ideal Timeline

7th to 9th Grade

> Complete or update diagnostic testing for the disability with a qualified evaluator, usually an educational psychologist or medical doctor. Ask for a complete report suitable for application for SAT or ACT accommodations.

Four to Six Months Before First Exam

> Submit application for accommodations to the College Board for PSAT 10, PSAT, SAT, or AP exams and to the ACT for the ACT exam.

Fall of Junior Year

> If you haven't before, submit application for accommodations to College Board and ACT. You'll need to register for the ACT before you apply.

Spring to Summer of Junior Year

> Begin practicing for the exams. Practice tends to help struggling learners even more than other students.
>
> Get fee waivers if you qualify.
>
> Register for the ACT and SAT.
>
> Take the ACT and SAT.
>
> Check the scores and decide which test to focus your practice on.
>
> Research colleges and develop a list to apply to.

Ask teachers, coaches, or club advisors if they'd be willing to write you a recommendation letter.

Fall of Senior Year

Get exam and application fee waivers if you qualify.

Register to take at least the test you scored best on in the spring one more time.

Ask recommenders to complete recommendation letters and to submit online when requested, but to also make several copies, seal each in an envelope, and sign across the seal so that you can mail them to colleges as needed.

Complete college applications and submit in time for scholarship deadlines.

Fill out FAFSA (and PROFILE, if needed) and submit.

Complete separate college scholarship applications, as directed on college sites.

Visit your top colleges, if you are able.

Wait and pray!

Spring of Senior Year

If invited to a scholarship competition or scholarship day, do not fail to attend or you will not get a scholarship.

As you receive acceptances, visit the colleges you are most interested in (or which offer you the best scholarships or aid) and visit the disability support services office.

Pray, discuss, pray some more and decide where to attend. Send in your deposit and commit to attend. They'll tell you what to do next, but be sure you contact the disability support office and let them know you are coming.

Fall of Freshman Year in College

Meet with disability support team and make a plan.

Meet with your professors and make a plan.

Work hard and succeed!

Resources

Note

Every effort has been made to use up-to-date links, but they may, of course, change at any time. If a resource is no longer at the listed link, search on that site for the title of the resource. An updated list of links will also be kept at https://www.raisingrealmen.com/helpupdate. Use the password bookaccess321.

Resources for SAT, PSAT, PSAT 10, and AP Exams

College Board Services for Students with Disabilities (SSD)

College Board SSD Program
P.O. Box 7504
London, KY 40742-7504

Phone: 212-713-8333
Toll Free: 844-255-7728
Fax: 866-360-0114
Email: ssd@info.collegeboard.org

Documentation needed for various disabilities

https://www.collegeboard.org/students-with-disabilities/documentation-guidelines/disability-documentation

Types of accommodations available

https://www.collegeboard.org/students-with-disabilities/typical-accommodations

Deadlines for each test date

https://www.collegeboard.org/students-with-disabilities/calendar

Student Eligibility Form

> https://secure-media.collegeboard.org/ssd/pdf/2018-sat-ssd-eligibility-form.pdf

SAT Practice Exams

> https://collegereadiness.collegeboard.org/sat/practice/full-length-practice-tests

Register for the SAT

> https://collegereadiness.collegeboard.org/sat/register

Resources for the ACT Exam

ACT Special Testing
301 ACT Drive, PO Box 4028
Iowa City, IA 52243

Phone: 319-337-1332
Fax: 319-341-2415
Email: actaccom@act.org

Register for the ACT

> https://www.act.org/content/act/en/products-and-services/the-act/registration.html

Request for ACT-Approved Accommodations

> https://www.act.org/content/dam/act/secured/documents/ACTAccoms-RequestForm.pdf

Exceptions Statement

> https://www.act.org/content/dam/act/unsecured/documents/ExceptionsStatementFormandChecklist.pdf

Teacher Survey Form

> https://www.act.org/content/dam/act/unsecured/documents/TeacherSurveyForm.pdf

Types of accommodations and testing infographic

https://www.act.org/content/dam/act/unsecured/documents/Accommodations-National-Special.pdf

ACT Policy for Accommodations Documentation

https://www.act.org/content/dam/act/unsecured/documents/6368-ACT-Policy-for-Documentation-Web.pdf

Checklist for Homeschoolers

https://www.act.org/content/dam/act/unsecured/documents/requesting-act-approved-accommodations-homeschool.pdf

ACT Practice Exam

https://www.act.org/content/dam/act/unsecured/documents/Preparing-for-the-ACT.pdf

Resources for the CLT Exam

Classic Learning Test Disability Requirements

https://www.cltexam.com/documents/ClassicLearningTestDisabilityRequirements.pdf

Register for the CLT

https://www.cltexam.com/register

Fee Waiver Resources

Income Eligibility Guidelines. Click on the proper year, then the pdf report, then scroll down until you see the chart for income eligibility guidelines. Include dependents listed on your taxes in household size.

https://www.fns.usda.gov/cacfp/income-eligibility-guidelines

Explanation of Fee Waivers from College Board. Print a copy to take with you.

https://blog.collegeboard.org/guide-to-sat-fee-waivers

ACT Fee Waiver Eligibility Handout. Print a copy to take with you.

https://www.act.org/content/dam/act/unsecured/documents/FeeWaiver.pdf

ACT College Application Fee Waivers. Print out four to take with you.

https://www.act.org/content/dam/act/unsecured/documents/RequestForWaiverForm.pdf

National Association of College Admission Counseling. Fee Waivers Print out four to take with you.

https://www.nacacfairs.org/globalassets/college-fair--homepage/ncf-documents/learn/student-application-fee-waiver-2018.pdf

Resources for Educational Plans

Anatomy of an IEP

https://www.understood.org/en/school-learning/special-services/ieps/at-a-glance-anatomy-of-an-iep

Contents of the IEP

https://www.parentcenterhub.org/iepcontents/

Possible Accommodations

Very thorough list of accommodations for ADHD (and learning disabilities)

https://www.additudemag.com/accommodations-iep-for-high-school-students/

Extensive list of accommodations for mitochondrial disease (and other medical issue) http://www.mitoaction.org/files/Suggested%20Accommodations%20for%20Middle%20and%20High%20School%20Students.pdf

Detailed list of accommodations for various disabilities

http://www.warmlinefrc.org/uploads/5/9/5/8/5958794/section_504_accomodations.pdf

Resources for Applying to College

College Search at College Board is the place to find whether colleges are safeties, matches, or reaches. Search for the college, then click Applying in the left sidebar. The selectivity will be listed about halfway down that page. Just below that, click SAT and ACT scores to look at the mid-range scores for admitted applicants.

https://bigfuture.collegeboard.org/find-colleges

The Common App is a college application program that allows you to apply to multiple colleges at once, so that you only have to separately do the unique parts for each school. A real time saver.

https://www.commonapp.org/

The Coalition App is a new college application program that allows you to apply to multiple colleges at once, so that you only have to separately do the unique parts for each school. A real time saver.

http://www.coalitionforcollegeaccess.org/

See Fee Waiver Resources for college application fee waiver links and the section entitled Affording All This to see how to use them.

An Editable Transcript Template is part of this free Homeschooling High School Resource pack available at our site.

https://www.raisingrealmen.com/welcome-podcast-listeners/

The FAFSA is the government financial aid application form, required by most colleges.

    https://studentaid.ed.gov/sa/fafsa

Reference explaining that small business assets should not be reported on the FAFSA.

    https://fafsa.ed.gov/help/fotw35cF4c.htm

The PROFILE is the College Board financial aid application form, required by some, mostly elite, colleges.

    https://cssprofile.collegeboard.org/

Financial Help with Diagnostic Testing

    HSLDA Compassion, formerly known as The Homeschool Foundation

        https://cssprofile.collegeboard.org/

    Also look for foundations connected to your child's particular diagnosis.

Sample Email to School Board Official

Dear _____,

I don't know if you remember us - we've conversed at _____ in the past.

I've had a problem and I wonder if you could help me.

As you may know, we homeschool our children. Over the years, we've had a friendly relationship with the guidance counselors at _____ High School. There are a few things that homeschoolers have to have the help of the public schools to accomplish. The College Board will not allow homeschool organizations to administer the PSAT, SAT, or AP exams. The ACT is the same.

This fall, I contacted the guidance counselor and asked to register our son for the PSAT. I received the following message:

_____

Hello, I hope this email finds you well.

I wanted to follow up on the discussion we had concerning whether or not your son would be able to take the AP or ACT exams at a _____ County school. After contacting the Director for Testing in _____ County Schools she verified we are not allowed to test a student on any test unless he/she is enrolled in our school.

I apologize for the inconvenience this may cause. Remember you can find ACT and testing dates and sites on a Saturday at a _____ County school on the testing websites.

Please let me know if I can help in any way.

_____

I was pretty shocked at this. We have done AP, ACT, and PSAT testing with the _____ County Schools for many years (at this time, three of our children have graduated from our homeschool and gone on to college). **We don't have any alternative! Homeschoolers are not allowed to administer these tests ourselves!**

As a taxpayer, I am equally upset. The taxes we pay into the system are far less than any expenditure the system undergoes for including our students in test administrations, especially since the College Board fees include an amount paid to the school for their administration.

I'm up a tree. I have a son that needs SAT and AP tests (and has to have College Board - approved accommodations as well). I don't know what to do. Why are homeschoolers now being excluded from testing?

Can you help us? I am at a loss.

Gratefully,

Hal & Melanie Young

Sample Simple Educational Plan

Your Homeschool Name
A Homeschool Registered with the Your State's Oversight Agency
Your Street Address, City, State, and Zip Code

Student Education Plan

Junior D. Student

SSN: 000-000-0000
Birthdate: 0/0/0000

Grade: 11

School Year: 2018-2019
Dates of Student Educational Plan: Date of K or 1st - Present
Date of Expected Graduation: 5/2020__

Diagnosed Disability: [Example: Learning Disability in the Area of Writing (DSM-IV-TR 315.9) and Learning Disability, Not Otherwise Specified (DSM-IV-TR 315.90)]

Latest Disability Testing
   Date: Date of Latest Test
   Administrator/Evaluator: Your Evaluator's Name and Credentials
   IQ Test: [Example: WISC-IV]
   Achievement Test: [Example: WJ-III NU{
   Additional Tests: [Examples: Nelson-Denny Reading Test (NDRT), Test of Written Language – Third Edition (TOWL-4), Beery-Buktenica Developmental Test of Visual Motor Integration (VMI)]

Previous Disability Testing
   10/24/2016, Evaluator name and company or credentials
   9/24/2011, Evaluator name and company or credentials
   6/24/2008, Evaluator name and company or credentials

Present Level of Educational Performance

Although Junior has made significant progress over the last several years, he continues to experience ongoing difficulties related to his diagnosed disabilities. His performance in reading is inconsistent. Sometimes he reads at an appropriate pace, while at other times he reads much more slowly than would be expected for his age. He is able to read and comprehend college level texts, but he needs extra time to do it in. His handwriting is still years below what one would expect, though his composition skills are far above average when he dictates. He is beginning to use a computer to type regularly. Again, his handwriting and processing speed mean that he struggles to complete his math work and tests, although his comprehension of math is excellent. He remains easily distracted and needing frequent breaks in the day. He is unable to both take notes and listen at the same time although his listening skills are above average and he remembers nearly everything he has heard. His grades are excellent with appropriate interventions.

Goals for Future Performance

Writing
- Work toward increased keyboarding skills.
- Improve spelling skills through visual, graphic illustration and modeling, such as Memverse.
- Continue to work on composition and editing skills.

Reading
- Junior will continue to work toward increased reading pace.

Math
- Junior will continue to review and work on retention of math concepts.
- Junior will complete Precalculus.
- Junior will work on increasing processing speed on math problems through drills and occasional timed assignments without grades.

Processing Speed & Academic Fluency
- Junior will continue to work on increasing his processing speed through challenging assignments and computer programs.

General Academics/All Subjects
- Junior will continue to strive to improve writing, reading, math, and processing skills as detailed in other sections.
- Junior will succeed in courses commensurate with his high intellectual ability, through accommodation and support of his needs and disabilities.

Transition
- Junior will continue an organized program of test preparation for college entry exams.
- Junior will complete composition and essay writing for college admissions essays.
- Junior will be given opportunities to role-play interview situations and college visits.
- Junior will choose a college or university to attend based on acceptances received.
- Junior will contact the chosen colleges Office of Disability Support Services and ask for accommodations.

Accommodations Allowed

Writing
- Junior will be allowed to dictate writing assignments to a scribe.
- Junior will be allowed to use a computer to complete writing assignments, as he is comfortable.
- Junior will receive extra time (up to double time) to complete assignments.
- Junior may take exams orally or dictated to a scribe.
- Junior may use a voice recorder to record lectures and assignments.

Reading
- Junior will be provided with CD recordings of his textbooks and reading material wherever possible, as well as hardcopy texts to allow for listening while reading along.
- Junior will be allowed to use a voice recorder to record lectures to allow for listening as a form of review.
- Junior will be allowed extended time (up to double) on tests and exams.

Math
- Junior will be given extended time to complete math assignments, tests, and exams.
- Junior may be given shorter assignments in math, as needed.
- Junior will be allowed to use a calculator on all math assignments, tests and exams.

Processing Speed & Academic Fluency
- Junior will be given extended time (up to double, or untimed) to complete assignments, tests, and exams.
- Junior will be testing in an alternate setting, if he believes it would help his performance.
- Junior will be given access to teacher's and other student's notes.
- Junior will be allowed to use a voice recorder.
- Junior will be allowed to mark directly in textbooks.
- Junior will be provided audios of his texts and additional readings whenever possible.

General Academics/All Subjects
- Junior will be allowed to use the accommodations listed in previous sections in every subject since high school subjects use multiple educational skills.

Transition
- Junior will be continue to be given one-on-one help in developing his resume and then college plans and applications next fall and counseling in considering admissions offers the next spring.
- Junior will be doing more college level work over the next year and he will be given one on one advising on strategies for success in college.
- Junior will be given help seeking adequate support for his learning disabilities as he transitions to college.

Help is on the Way

Sample Detailed Educational Plan (Seldom Necessary)

Your Homeschool Name
A Homeschool Registered with the Your State's Oversight Agency
Your Street Address, City, State, and Zip Code

Student Education Plan

Junior D. Student

SSN: 000-000-0000
Birthdate: 0/0/0000

Grade: 11

School Year: 2018-2019
Dates of Student Educational Plan: Date of K or 1st - Present
Date of Expected Graduation: 5/2020_

Diagnosed Disability: [Example: Learning Disability in the Area of Writing (DSM-IV-TR 315.9) and Learning Disability, Not Otherwise Specified (DSM-IV-TR 315.90)]

Latest Disability Testing
  Date: Date of Latest Test
  Administrator/Evaluator: Your Evaluator's Name and Credentials
  IQ Test: [Example: WISC-IV]
  Achievement Test: [Example: WJ-III NU{
  Additional Tests: [Examples: Nelson-Denny Reading Test (NDRT), Test of Written Language – Third Edition (TOWL-4), Beery-Buktenica Developmental Test of Visual Motor Integration (VMI)]

Previous Disability Testing
  10/24/2016, Evaluator name and company or credentials
  9/24/2011, Evaluator name and company or credentials
  6/24/2008, Evaluator name and company or credentials

Writing
  Functional Limitations
    Diagnosis: Learning Disability in the Area of Writing (DSM-IV-TR 315.9)

    Testing: WJ-III NU 11/7/2016

Broad Written Language	<Numerical results>
Brief Writing	<Numerical results>
Writing Expression	<Numerical results>
Spelling	<Numerical results>
Writing Fluency	<Numerical results>
Writing Juniors	<Numerical results>

Testing: TOWL-4 11/7/2016

Spontaneous Writing	<Numerical results>

Contextual Conventions	<Numerical results>
Story Construction	<Numerical results>

Testing: From evaluation 11/7/2016: "Junior is displaying significant issues in the area of writing...Junior's writing abilities are significantly lower than what would be expected based on his cognitive abilities...He also has difficulty with fine motor control. This most likely will cause him to have great difficulty writing...He will benefit from being given the opportunity to keyboard or dictate instead of write..."

Accommodations
- Junior will be allowed to dictate writing assignments to a scribe.
- Junior will be allowed to use a computer to complete writing assignments, as he is comfortable.
- Junior will receive extra time (up to double time) to complete assignments.
- Junior may take exams orally or dictated to a scribe.
- Junior may use a voice recorder to record lectures and assignments.

Goals
- Work toward increased keyboarding skills.
- Improve spelling skills through visual, graphic illustration and modeling, such as Memverse.
- Continue to work on composition and editing skills.

Reading
Functional Limitations
Impacted by Learning Disability, Not Otherwise Specified (DSM-IV-TR 315.90) and previous diagnosis of Learning Disability in the Area of Reading

Testing: WISC-IV 11/7/2016

Verbal Comprehension	<Numerical results>
Similarities	<Numerical results>
Vocabulary	<Numerical results>
Comprehension	<Numerical results>

Testing: WISC-IV 11/7/2016

Processing Speed	<Numerical results>
Coding	<Numerical results>
Symbol Search	<Numerical results>

Testing: WJ-III NU 11/7/2016

Broad Reading	<Numerical results>
Letter-Word Identification	<Numerical results>
Reading Fluency	<Numerical results>
Passage Comprehension	<Numerical results>

Testing: From Evaluation 11/7/2016 "Junior's reading abilities are somewhat inconsistent...He reads at a very slow pace on some tasks yet at a typical pace on other tasks. He should be offered extended time during reading tests to ensure he has as much time as he needs."

Accommodations
- Junior will be provided with CD recordings of his textbooks and reading material wherever possible, as well as hardcopy texts to allow for listening while reading along.
- Junior will be allowed to use a voice recorder to record lectures to allow for listening as a form of review.
- Junior will be allowed extended time (up to double) on tests and exams.

Goals
- Junior will be tutored in the SQ4R approach to reading.
- Junior will continue to work toward increased reading pace.
- Junior will continue to work toward increased comprehension.

Math

Functional Limitations

Impacted by Learning Disability, Not Otherwise Specified (DSM-IV-TR 315.90)

Testing: WISC-IV 11/7/2016

Processing Speed	<numerical result>
Coding	<numerical result>
Symbol Search	<numerical result>

Testing: WJ-III NU 11/7/2016

Broad Mathematics	<numerical result>
Calculation	<numerical result>
Math Fluency	<numerical result>
Applied Problems	<numerical result>

Testing: From Evaluation 11/7/2016: "Junior displays a significant slowness in the speed in which he is able to complete math tasks (math fluency). This may impede upon his ability to complete math assignments and math tests in a timely manner.

Accommodations
- Junior will be given extended time to complete math assignments, tests, and exams.
- Junior may be given shorter assignments in math, as needed.
- Junior will be allowed to use a calculator on all math assignments, tests and exams.

Goals
- Junior will continue to review and work on retention of math concepts.
- Junior will complete Precalculus.
- Junior will work on increasing processing speed on math problems through drills and occasional timed assignments without grades.

Processing Speed & Academic Fluency

Functional limitations

Diagnosis: Learning Disability, Not Otherwise Specified (DSM-IV-TR 315.90)

Testing: WISC-IV 11/7/2016

Processing Speed	<numerical result>
Coding	<numerical result>
Symbol Search	<numerical result>

Testing: WJ-III NU

Academic Skills	<numerical result>
Academic Fluency	<numerical result>
Academic Application	<numerical result>

Testing: From Evaluation 11/7/2016 "Cognitive functioning was evaluated with regard to processing speed. This is a weakness for Junior with scores falling much lower than expected. This makes it difficult to take notes quickly enough and hard to finish tests in a timely manner. Junior's overall cognitive abilities fall within the superior range, so one would predict that his academic skills would also fall within that range, but Junior has difficulty completing tasks quickly...These findings suggest that he processes information more slowly than would be expected for his age, he may not catch all the instructions, and he may be slow at copying down information.

Accommodations
- Junior will be given extended time (up to double, or untimed) to complete assignments, tests, and exams.
- Junior will be testing in an alternate setting, if he believes it would help his performance.
- Junior will be given access to teacher's and other student's notes.
- Junior will be allowed to use a voice recorder.
- Junior will be allowed to mark directly in textbooks.
- Junior will be provided audios of his texts and additional readings whenever possible.

Goals
- Junior will continue to work on increasing his processing speed through challenging assignments and computer programs.

General Academics/All Subjects
Functional limitations
Diagnosis: Learning Disability in the Area of Writing (DSM-IV-TR 315.9)
Diagnosis: Learning Disability, Not Otherwise Specified (DSM-IV-TR 315.90)

Junior's diagnosed learning disabilities present him with functional limitations in the areas of writing, reading, math and processing speed that will impact him in all of his academic subjects. Please refer to test scores above for documentation.

Accommodations
- Junior will be allowed extended time (up to double or untimed) on assignments, tests, and exams.
- Junior will be allowed to dictate or keyboard (if he is comfortable) assignments, tests and exams.
- Junior will be allowed to use voice recognition software to complete assignments.

- Junior may be tested orally, where appropriate.
- Junior will be provided with a quiet or isolated testing environment when requested.
- Junior will be provided with his texts and additional readings in audio CD or mp3 wherever possible.
- Junior will be allowed to use a voice recorder to record lectures and assignments.
- Junior will be provided with teacher and student notes where needed.

Goals

- Junior will continue to strive to improve writing, reading, math, and processing skills as detailed in other sections.
- Junior will succeed in courses commensurate with his high intellectual ability, through accommodation and support of his needs and disabilities.

Transition

Junior has expressed career goals which would necessitate higher education and is interested in attending a four year university. His intellectual ability is commensurate with that goal given adequate support for his learning disabilities.

Testing: WISC-IV 11/7/2016

Verbal Comprehension	<numerical result>
Similarities	<numerical result>
Vocabulary	<numerical result>
Comprehension	<numerical result>

Testing: WISC-IV 11/7/2016

Full Scale Score	<numerical result>
General Ability Index	<numerical result>

Accommodations

- Junior will be continue to be given one-on-one help in developing his resume and then college plans and applications next fall and counseling in considering admissions offers the next spring.
- Junior will be doing more college level work over the next year and he will be given one on one advising on strategies for success in college.
- Junior will be given help seeking adequate support for his learning disabilities as he transitions to college.

Goals

Junior will continue an organized program of test preparation for college entry exams.
Junior will complete composition and essay writing for college admissions essays.
Junior will be given opportunities to role-play interview situations and college visits.
Junior will choose a college or university to attend based on acceptances received.
Junior will contact the chosen colleges Office of Disability Support Services and ask for accommodations.

Conclusion

Junior has made remarkable progress in the past several years, from an inability to read at age 10, to reading at grade level and functioning at a high school level academically. He continues to need extensive accommodations, particularly in written communication and processing time. Our general goals are to continue to prepare him for success in college, while teaching him coping mechanisms and work-arounds for his disabilities.

Sample Educational Plan for Medical Accommodations

Your Homeschool's Name
Registered with the Your State Division of Non-Public Education
Street Address, City, State Zip

Student Educational/Medical Plan

Jane Q. Student
SSN: ***-**-****
Birthdate: 01/01/2005

Grade: 11

School Year: 2022-2023
Dates of Student Educational Plan:
06/2011 -Present
Date of Expected Graduation: 5/2024__

Diagnosed Disability: Hypermobile Ehlers Danlos Syndrome, ICD-10 Q79.62

Latest Medical Assessment
    Date: 01/26/2023
    Administrator/Evaluator: Joe R. Doctor, M.D.
    Diagnostic Test: Diagnostic Criteria for Hypermobile Ehlers-Danlos Syndrome (heDS) by The International Consortium on Ehlers-Danlos Syndromes and Related Disorders
    Additional Tests: Connective Tissue Disorders Panel, March 2022

Present Level of Educational Performance and Functional Limitations

Jane is a gifted musician and writer. She is very intellectually capable. She has participated in classes consisting primarily of university students and not only held her own but excelled.

Her medical situation, though, greatly impacts her schooling. Sometimes she can function normally, while other times she is severely impacted. She struggles to write for more than a few minutes, due to finger pain. Frequent migraines impact her ability to focus and read, particularly on a time schedule. Her recurrent joint dislocations, subluxations, and injuries impact her attendance and performance, due to pain. She must be able to shift positions, take breaks, have access to food, drink, and meds, and is sometimes limited in her mobility and activity.

It is important to note that Jane's condition varies from day to day. Some days she will need all the accommodations and still struggle to function through her level of pain, while on other days, fewer accommodations will be needed. When not wearing braces or using a wheelchair, Jane can appear healthy, despite experiencing many days on which her pain level is 6-8 out of 10. Care should be taken not to make assumptions about her level of pain. Because of this, it is important to allow her to decide what she is able to do as a highly gifted student who is committed to succeed.

Goals for Future Performance

Jane's primary goals for future educational performance involve continuing to learn how to manage her illness and develop work-arounds and accommodations that will allow her to continue to excel and reach the full potential of her talents.

Accommodations Allowed

Writing

- Jane will be offered extended time (up to double time) and flexible deadlines to complete writing assignments due to hand pain.
- Jane will be allowed to use alternatives to writing, such as dictation to a scribe, oral exams, speech recognition software, a voice recorder, or a notetaker.
- Jane will be allowed to use a computer to complete assignments, as tolerated.

Reading

- Jane will be provided with audio recordings or a reader wherever possible, to allow for listening when reading is difficult due to migraines.
- Jane will be allowed to use a voice recorder to record lectures to allow for listening as a form of review.
- Jane will be allowed extended time (up to double) on tests and exams, to allow for distraction due to pain and migraines.

Math

- Jane will be given extended time to complete math assignments, tests, and exams, due to hand pain and distraction due to pain.
- Jane may be given shorter assignments in math, as needed.
- Jane will be allowed to use a calculator on all math assignments, tests and exams, to reduce the need for writing.

General Academics/All Subjects

- Jane will be allowed to use the accommodations listed in previous sections in every subject since high school subjects use multiple educational skills.
- Jane will be tested in an quiet or isolated setting, if needed to avoid migraines.
- Jane will be given access to teacher's and student's notes, due to difficulty writing.
- Jane should be allowed excused unexplained absences or to arrive late or leave early, due to medical issues.
- Jane should be allowed to take medications in class and have access to food and water.
- Jane should be given flexible deadlines, as she may sometimes be too sick to work.
- Jane's schedule should allow extra time to travel between classes.
- Jane should have access to hot and cold packs during classes and exams, if needed.
- Jane may need to stand, move around, or change chairs to prevent pain.
- Jane will be allowed to decide when or if she can tolerate physical activity.
- Jane will be excused from physical education requirements unless the instructor is trained in safe exercise techniques for hEDS patients.

Transition

- Jane will be given one-on-one help in developing her resume, college plans, and applications next fall and counseling in considering admissions offers the next spring.
- Jane will be doing more college level work over the next year and she will be given one-on-one advising on strategies for success in college.
- Jane will be given help seeking adequate support for her medical disabilities as she transitions to college.

Conclusion

When Jane receives the appropriate accommodations, her performance is outstanding, despite her physical challenges. She is a musician with great promise, who will succeed if given the help she needs.

Sample Doctor's Letter for Medical Accommodations

Letter of Medical Necessity for Accommodations
Regarding JANE HOMESCHOOLER

To Whom It May Concern:

This letter is in regard to one of our patients, Jane Homeschooler (birthdate 1/1/2005). Jane has Hypermobile Ehlers-Danlos Syndrome, a genetic connective tissue disorder involving a defect in collagen production. "Characteristic symptoms of hEDS include joint hypermobility and instability, recurrent joint subluxations or dislocations, chronic widespread joint pain, skin manifestations, and a wide variety of associated symptoms and comorbidities, including migraine headaches, functional bowel disorders, orthostatic intolerance, and chronic fatigue, among many others." (Am J Med Genet A. 2019 Apr; 179(4): 561–569). The symptoms of this disease are often intermittent from day to day and it is impossible to predict when flares of the disease may occur.

Jane, a bright and musically gifted young woman, has been under my care since birth. Her family, part of our practice for over twenty years, has a history of hypermobility and joint instability. Jane has a history of joint instability and joint dislocations in the absence of trauma dating back to toddlerhood. In the preteen years, she repeatedly rolled her ankles and subluxed her knees, resulting in several fractures. In adolescence, Jane has evidenced chronic pain and fatigue, recurrent joint instability, hyperextension, and subluxations, chronic intractable migraines, recurrent nausea, dizziness, and fainting. Through this time, Jane has seen or has appointments scheduled with specialists in Genetics, Cardiology, Neurology, Orthopedics, Rheumatology, and Physical Therapy.

Diagnosed Disability: Hypermobile Ehlers-Danlos Syndrome (hEDS), also known as: Ehlers-Danlos Syndrome, Type 3, ICD-10 Q79. 62; Chronic Migraine with Aura, ICD-10 G43.1; Postural Orthostatic Tachycardia Syndrome ICD-10 G90.A; Asthma ICD-10 J45.909.
    Latest Assessment: 05/01/2023
    Diagnostic Criteria: Diagnostic Criteria for Hypermobile Ehlers-Danlos Syndrome (hEDS) by The International Consortium on Ehlers-Danlos Syndromes and Related Disorders
    Results: Criterion I – Generalized Joint Hypermobility: (Beighton Score ≥5 required) Score 9/9;

Criterion II – Two or more of the following features (A, B, or C) must be present: Feature A (≥5 required) Score 6/12, Feature C (≥1 required), Score 3/3; Criterion III: Required exclusion met or further testing ordered.
Additional Tests: Genetic Connective Tissue Disorders Panel, 3/22; Echocardiogram, 6/22, Cranial CT Scan, 6/22; Opthalmology Assessment 7/22, Duke Genetics Assessment, 8/22; Dysautonomia Tilt Table Test, 6/23.
Medications/Interventions: Propranolol, Etodolac, Zolmitriptan, Sumatriptan, Nurtec, Albuterol, Epipen, Omeprazole, Reyvow, Ubrelvy, Ajovy, Migrelief supplement, Cusack Protocol supplements, Pycnogenol, Splints and Braces, Mobility Aids

Functional Limitations

Jane experiences recurrent joint dislocations and subluxations, and widespread and chronic pain, particularly involving her hands, knees, neck, and back. Sometimes she is able to function normally, while other times she is unable to walk for long distances or needs the use of mobility aids, such as crutches or a wheelchair. Her pain limits her ability to write for extended periods. She must frequently rest and needs extra sleep. She needs access to medications. Pain may limit her activities at times.

Jane has frequent, chronic migraines, causing visual disturbances, pain, fatigue, and brain fog. When symptomatic, she needs access to a quiet and dark room, prescribed migraine medications, and relaxed attendance requirements. She may be unable to read or to navigate when experiencing migraine aura.

Jane has irritable bowel syndrome, frequent nausea, lightheadedness, and dizziness. She needs access to food and drink when she feels necessary. Her condition is exacerbated by irritants and allergens and requires access to medications and must be able to leave triggering environments.

Accommodations
Academic
Jane should be offered extended time or flexible deadlines to complete writing assignments and alternatives to writing, such as a notetaker, dictation, computer-use, oral exams, speech recognition software, and voice recorder.

Jane should be given access to a reader or audiobooks for use when migraine with aura makes reading difficult.

Jane should be allowed excused unexplained absences or to arrive late or leave early, due to pain, asthma, or migraines. She should be allowed to take medications in class. She should be given flexible deadlines, as she may sometimes be too sick to work. She may need a quiet or isolated testing environment to prevent migraines. In examinations or timed assignments, Jane may need extra breaks to take medication or take food or drink.

Jane's schedule should allow extra time between classes and to group classes to make them easier to reach, so priority registration is helpful.

Jane should be allowed access to her food and drink, even in class, to prevent lightheadedness. She should have access to hot and cold packs during classes and exams, if needed. She may need to stand, move around, or change chairs occasionally to prevent pain.

Non-Academic
Although she is encouraged to remain active and exercise, Jane must be allowed to decide when or if she can tolerate physical activity. She may need to use braces, splints, crutches, a wheelchair, and medications as her pain, asthma, and injury level requires. Jane should be excused from physical education requirements unless the instructor is trained in safe exercise techniques for hEDS patients because lifelong damage can occur.

In a residential or college environment, Jane will need a centrally located, first-floor room, because of mobility and pain issues, a single room, due to need for darkness during migraines and increased need for sleep, and an un-lofted bed. She may need a tray or help with dishes in dining. Jane will need a car on campus for pharmacy and doctor visits and transportation on high pain days, as well as handicapped parking spaces near her room and classes.

Jane should be allowed to bring her service dog with her wherever she goes to alert her to an imminent migraine in time to take medication and to help her with other trained tasks.

Joe Q Doctor, M.D.
Company Family Medicine
Address
Address
Phone

Traditionally Organized Transcript

Your Homeschool's Name
A Homeschool Registered with the [State Agency] in [Your State]
1111 Your Street, Your Town, NC 11111
919-111-1111

John Q. Student
SSN: 111-11-1111
Date of Birth: 01/01/2001

[Anticipated] Graduation Date: 5/24/11
Class Rank: N/A

Parents: Joe & Jill Homeschooler
Dates Enrolled: 9/2005 – Present

9th Grade 2015-16

Course	Credit	Grade
Grammar & Composition	1.0	B
Great Books I History	1.0	A
Economics*	0.5	A
U.S. Government	0.5	A
Algebra I	1.0	B
Honors Biology with Lab	1.0	B
Band: Saxophone*	0.5	A
Chorus*	0.5	A

10th Grade 2016-2017

Course	Credit	Grade
English Literature*	1.0	A
U.S. History	1.0	B
Philosophy*	0.5	A
French I: Conversation*	1.0	B
Geometry	1.0	A
Honors Chemistry with Lab	1.0	A
Band: Saxophone*	0.5	A
Chorus*	0.5	A

11th Grade 2017-2018

Course	Credit	Grade
European Literature	1.0	A
European History	1.0	A
AP Comparative Government	0.5	B
French II: Conversation & Reading	1.0	B
Honors Algebra II	1.0	A
Honors Physics with Lab	1.0	A
Music Performance*	0.5	A

12th Grade 2018-2019

Course	Credit	Grade
English Language	1.0	~
World History	1.0	~
French III	1.0	~
Honors Precalculus	1.0	~
AP Chemistry with Lab*,**	1.0	~
Senior Honors Research Project	0.5	~
Music Performance*	0.5	~
Christian Thought	1.0	~

High School Courses Completed Prior to High School

Course	Grade
Physical Science with Lab	A
Latin	B

Test Scores

Test	Date	Score
AP English Language	5/10	5
AP Chemistry	5/10	4

Award of Some Kind, 2007

Highest SAT Scores

Area	Verbal	Math	Writing
Score	XXX	XXX	XXX
Dates	3/10, 10/10	5/10	10/10

Grade Point Average

Unweighted	3.71
Weighted	4.02
Credits Earned	25.5

Weighted GPA adds one quality point for Honors and two for AP courses, as the Your State Board of Education Policy Manual recommends.

*Class either partially or entirely taught by outside instructor.
**As required by the College Board, all AP courses have been authorized to use the AP designation.
~ Course in Progress, no grade issued yet.

I, Joseph P. HomeschoolDad, do hereby certify and affirm that this is the official transcript and academic record of John Q. Student for the years of 2015-2019.

Administrator: _____
Joseph P. HomeschoolDad

Date: _____

©2010 Hal and Melanie Young
Permission is granted for workshop attendees, CD or mp3 purchasers, or subscribers to copy, imitate, and personalize for their own transcripts. Permission to publish on the internet, by photocopy, by email, or elsewhere is not granted. **This notice may be removed only for your student's official transcript.**

Transcript by Subject

Your Homeschool Name
A Homeschool Registered with Your State's Oversight Agency
Your Street Address, State, Zip
Your Phone Number

Junior D. Student
SSN: 000-00-0000
Date of Birth: 01/01/2001

[Anticipated] Graduation Date: 6/1/2019
Class Rank: N/A

Parents: Dad & Mom Student
Dates Enrolled: 9/2005 – Current

English Courses

Course	Credit	Grade	Year
Great Books I: Ancient Lit	1.0	A	FR
Honors English Composition*	1.0	A	SO
Honors American Literature	1.0	A	JR
Honors Great Books II	1.0	~	SR

Math Courses

Course	Credit	Grade	Year
Honors Algebra I	1.0	A	FR
Honors Algebra II	1.0	A	SO
Honors Geometry	1.0	A	JR
Honors Precalculus	1.0	~	SR

Science Courses

Course	Credit	Grade	Year
Honors Physical Science	1.0	A	FR
Honors Biology	1.0	A	SO
Honors Chemistry*	1.0	A	JR
AP Chemistry with Lab**	1.0	~	SR

History and Social Sciences Courses

Course	Credit	Grade	Year
Great Books I: Ancient History	1.0	A	FR
Great Books II: Medieval	1.0	A	SO
Great Books III: Explorers	1.0	A	JR
Dual Enrollment Politics*	1.0	A	JR
AP U.S. History**	1.0	~	SR

Other Courses

Course	Credit	Grade	Year
Physical Education	0.5	A	FR
Music: Concert Band	0.5	A	FR
Business I	0.5	A	FR
Business II	0.5	A	SO
Business III	0.5	A	JR
Senior Business Course	1.0	~	SR

Foreign Language Courses

Course	Credit	Grade	Year
American Sign Language I	1.0	B	FR
American Sign Language II	1.0	A	SO
Spanish I	1.0	A	JR
Spanish II	1.0	~	SR

SAT Scores

Area	Verbal	Math
Score	XXX	XXX
Dates	6/18	10/18

Awaiting scores from 10/4 administration

ACT Scores

Area	Composite	Reading	Math
Score	XX	XX	XX
Dates	6/18	6/18	6/18

Planning to test 10/27

Grade Point Average

Unweighted	3.95
Weighted	4.22
Credits Earned	18.5
Credits in Progress	6

Weighted GPA adds one-half quality point for Honors and one for AP or college level courses.

*Class either partially or entirely taught by outside instructor.
**As required by the College Board, all AP courses have been authorized to use the AP designation.
~ Course In-Progress

I, Father D. Student, do hereby certify and affirm that this is the official transcript and academic record of Junior D. Student for the years of 2015-2018.

Administrator: _____
Father D. Student

Date: _____

©2018 Hal and Melanie Young
Permission is granted for workshop attendees, CD or mp3 purchasers, or subscribers to copy, imitate, and personalize for their own transcripts. Permission to publish on the internet, by photocopy, by email, or elsewhere is not granted. **This notice may be removed only for your student's official transcript.**

Help is on the Way

Other Books by Hal & Melanie Young

No Longer Little: Parenting Tweens with Grace and Hope

Raising Real Men: Surviving, Teaching, and Appreciating Boys

Love, Honor, and Virtue: Gaining or Regaining a Biblical Attitude Toward Sexuality'

My Beloved and My Friend: How to be Married to Your Best Friend Without Changing Spouses

Christ-Centered Christmas

Christ-Centered Advent

Christ-Centered Thanksgiving

Reformation Day: Finding Christ in History

Find our books at www.RaisingRealMen.com/shop

www.ingramcontent.com/pod-product-compliance
Lightning Source LLC
Chambersburg PA
CBHW081501070526
44586CB00019B/2454